FRENCH MINOR RAILWAYS VOL 2

Peter Smith

COPYRIGHT 2014 PETER SMITH

ISBN-13: 978-1494911133

ISBN-10: 1494911132

CHAPTERS

CHAPTER 1	CdF d'Ille et Vilaine.	3
CHAPTER 2	Rive de Gier tramway	13
CHAPTER 3	Revigny	23
CHAPTER 4	Dompierre to Abbeville	40
CHAPTER 5	Maule to Versailles tramway	53
CHAPTER 6	The line of the Emperors	65
CHAPTER 7	Voiron	72
CHAPTER 8	Lagny to Mortcerf tramway	80
CHAPTER 9	Chamaret to Taulignan tramway	88

In this second volume of French Minor Railways I have again tried to present a selection of lines that are little known yet repay study in so many ways….there are lines in the mountains, lines in the flatlands around Paris, a line running into Versailles and another that was for the sole use of the Emperor. I have included all the pictures that I can find, nearly all of them from old postcards from the 1900 to 1914 period when thankfully the village or town station was one of the features the local postcard photographer always tried to include. Without them many of these lines would have disappeared into the mists of time….a lot of them closed beyond living memory and traces on the ground are few. Many of them simply ran along the verge of a convenient road so trying to trace the route is all but impossible, especially if road improvements have taken place since the line closed. The postcards are a lifeline, our window into a vanished age when the speed of a metre gauge train was as fast as most people needed to travel.

CHAPTER 1 ANTRAIN TO LIFFRE   CdF d'Ille et Vilaine.

The trains from Antrain ran through to Rennes, the hub of the Tramways d'Ille et Vilaine, but this section of the line has enough interest without venturing into the big city. Antrain is a small town in Brittany, 50km east of St Malo and 45km north of Rennes; the population today is only 1400 so it was never a major destination in it's own right.

The Ille et Vilaine metre gauge network was extensive, this line running north from Rennes to terminate at Artrain where there was also a main line station on the Etat system. The tramway left the line to Fougeres at Liffre, and there was another junction station at Sens de Bretagne where a branch headed off towards Pleine—Fougeres.

The stations were varied, and the provision at the junctions was often no more lavish than at the smallest villages. At Antrain the line terminated at Antrain Ouest outside the Etat station, convenient for passenger transfer, and the route by the tramway to Rennes was far more direct than by the main line railway even if it may not have been quicker or more comfortable. There was also a station in the town centre called Antrain Ville.

Leaving Antrain, stations served small villages at Tremblay, Rimoux, Romazy and then Sens en Bratagne which was the junction for the line to Pleine-Fourges which opened in 1905. Beyond Sens the line served Sautoger, Gahard and Erce pres Liffre before reaching the junction station of Liffre, 35km from Antrain.

The Antrain line was opened in 1903 and only ran until 1937. It was operated with a mixture of Corpet Louvet 030 tank loco's and Blanc Misseron Bicabine engines; one of the former, no. 75, is preserved.

This chapter will as far as possible illustrate the line using old postcards, though some of the stations seem to have escaped being photographed altogether.

This is the little terminus at Antrain Ville, with one of the Corpet Louvet loco's shunting the stock of a mixed train. The loading platform alongside the goods shed is served from a wagon turntable.

A Corpet Louvet tank running light engine away from the station at Antrain Ouest, out of sight on the right, towards the town and Antrain Ville. The Etat line is in the foreground.

There are rather more pictures of the Etat station that there are of the tramway, sadly. Perhaps not surprisingly this has also now closed and the nearest main line station is 10km away at Pontorosn; three stations for a town of under 1400 people was verging on the absurd.

Côte d'Emeraude — 1962. ANTRAIN — Intérieur de la Gare

Je Pars D'Antrain — Amitiés
1. - ANTRAIN-s/-COUESNON — Vue générale

Back to the tramway; leaving Antrain the next station along the line was at the village of Tremblay. Here in common with all the smaller stations a wooden station building sufficed. A siding runs off at right angles in front of the building, accessed from a turntable. The building design was used widely on the I&V system at the small stations.

This is the station serving Sens en Bretagne; the stations at Rimoux and Romazy seem to have escaped the photographer but were almost certainly very similar to Tremblay.

Sens station was very similar to Antrain, with a stone built station building and a wooden goods shed attached to it. The crane wagon on the left is standing on a siding reached from a wagon turntable which were a feature of the stations on the I&V. Sens was the junction for the line to Pleine-Fougeres.

Note the water crane, with a wooden barrel to catch the drips.

The station approach road can be seen to the right of the building. The brick built toilets look to be a later addition to the stone structure.

A last look at Sens with three trains in the station; these country junctions would have a brief period of intense activity and then nothing more would happen until the next trains were due, perhaps a couple of hours later. The track plan is basically four loops connected by the wagon turntables and the goods siding at right angles, the junction itself being beyond the station. There was a loco shed on the left behind the photographer, visible in the first photo of Sens.

The train on the left has a Blanc Misserton Bicabine locomotive, while the one in the centre has a Corpet Louvet 030.

I have no pictures of Santoger station but at least this picture was taken in the village.

9

There are also no pictures of Gahard, but the bridge carrying the tramway over the River Grette can be seen on the right.

Below, one of the Corpet Louvet tanks is running alongside the road towards the junction station at Liffre.

1 LA BRETAGNE. — Liffré (I.-et-V.). — En Forêt.   J. Sorel, Éditeur, Rennes

This section ran through a heavily wooded and very attractive area; one of the Blanc Misseron loco's heads a passenger train.

On May 16th 1910 a three coach train was comprehensively demolished in this accident to a train returning from a flower festival in Rennes and twenty nine people were hurt. Remarkably the glass in the door on the right is still unbroken.

LA BRETAGNE   13. LIFFRÉ (Ille-et-Vilaine) — Déraillement du Tramway au retour de la fête des Fleurs de Rennes

Liffre was a junction station but one of the small wooden station buildings was all it received. Timber traffic seems to be important; the usual siding connected by turntables runs behind the station building. The station looks fairly scruffy with old posters having been removed from the end wall.

This verdant goods yard scene is at Erce, the next station north of Liffre, but the arrangement using turntables seems to have been common to all the smaller stations. The wagon mounted cranes were a cheaper alternative to providing a fixed crane at each station.

CHAPTER 2 THE ST ETIENNE TO RIVE DE GIER TRAMWAY

St Etienne was the first city in France to construct a system of urban tramways; planned in 1879 the first line opened on December 4th 1881, operated with horse drawn trams, and the tramways have operated continuously ever since. The lines soon converted to steam power using locomotives supplied by Winterthur of Geneva, and the system grew larger at regular intervals. Electrification began in 1907 but it is the earlier period using steam trams that I want to illustrate here using the line to Rive de Gier which opened on November 16th 1882, the last of the first group of routes to open.

This was no mere urban tramway trundling around the city streets; Rive de Gier is 24km from St Etienne, this was a proper long distance route which served the villages of St Jean Bonnefonds, La Varizelle and La Grande Croix en route as well as the town of St Chamond.

One of the very distinctive original locomotives built in 1882 for the tramways; for the longer distance lines larger 030 locomotives would certainly have been used.

SAINT-ÉTIENNE. - Place Badouillère

9 RIVE-DE-GIER. — Arrêt du Train. — Faubourg d'Égarande. — LL.

This is the attractive terminus in Rive de Gier, with the wooden station building on the right under the trees. The tram locomotive ta taking on water; the station was simply a halt at the roadside from which the line ran right through the streets of the town as seen below.

RIVE-DE-GIER. - Rue de Lyon

This appears to be one of the little 0-4-0 loco's so they did run right out as far as Rive de Gier at least occasionally.

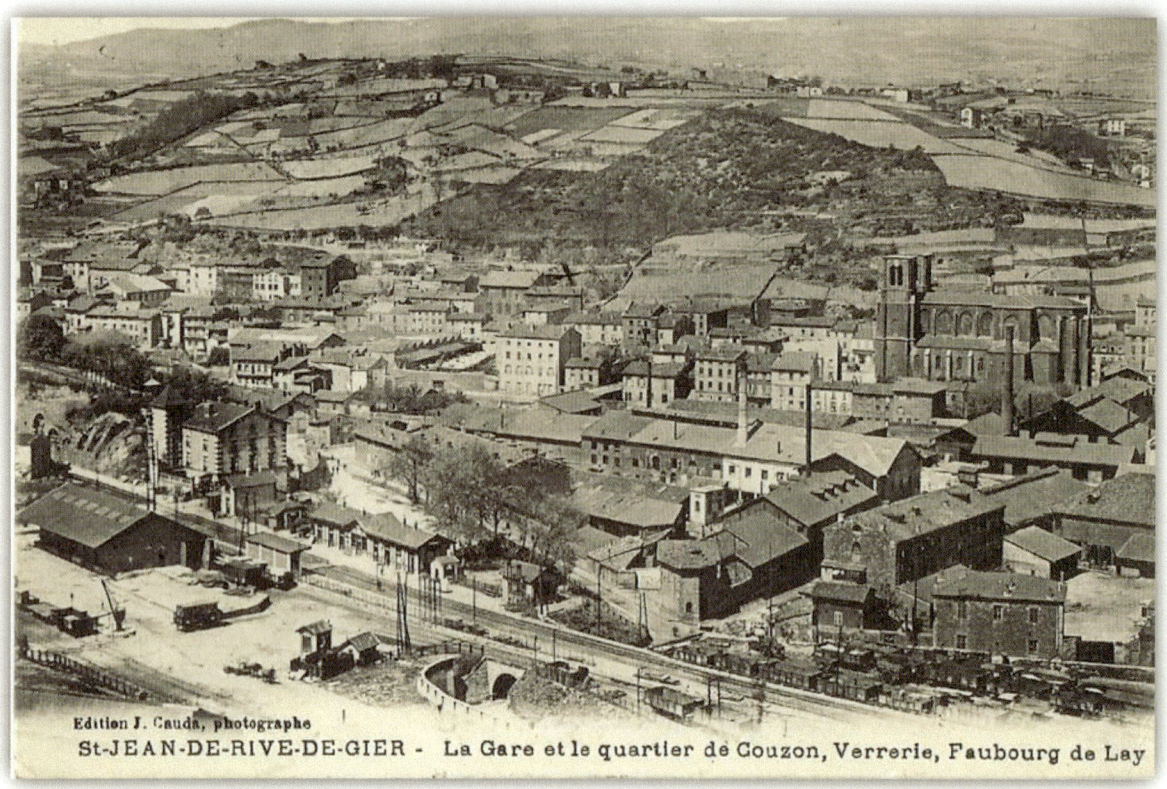

A panoramic view of Rive de Gier with a standard gauge line in the foreground.

Below is the main line station which was served by the tramway…..the main line was opened on 1st October 1830 between Lyon & St Etienne, a remarkably early route engineered by Marc and Camille Seguin.

This later picture taken after electrification shows the relationship of the tramway to the PLM station. Rive de Gier was an industrial town as the bottom picture shows. The station is below the smoking chimney; the tramway ran along the street outside.

The interior of the PLM station, showing the very short section of overall roof.

Below is a view over the PLM goods yard.

The only intermediate place of any size was Saint Chamond as seen here with a tramway train on the left. .

This is the PLM station which was served by the tramway.

Below, two trains can be seen passing in the street in the centre of the picture, on quite a steep gradient.

Taken after electrification, this view shows that the trams reversed at the PLM station before continuing their journey, something far easier with an electric tramcar.

This Winterthur built loco preserved in Switzerland is very similar to the larger 0-6-0 engines used on the tramway.

CHAPTER 3   LONS-LE-SAUNIER TO REVIGNY

This section of the line between Lons and Saint Claude was part of the first route on the extensive Jura narrow gauge system to be opened, in 1898. It was known as the CfV, the Compagnie Générale des Chemins de Fer Vicinaux and operated two systems, in Jura and in Haute Saône. Part of the Jura system was electrically operated but here we are concerned with the steam tramway that traversed some of the most dramatic scenery in France on the Jura plateau. The whole journey from Lons-le-Saunier to Saint Claude took about four hours on a good day; there was a proposal to rebuild the line to standard gauge as part of a Paris to Geneva trunk route but the advent of World War One finished that idea, not to mention the effect of actually working out the likely cost!

The tramway remained a tramway, though one with impressive infrastructure to get though the high areas and that is the reason for focussing on the section as far as Revingy, because it was dramatic in the extreme.   Unfortunately that could not save it from the inevitable end of all such lines, defeated by improved roads...it staggered on through World War Two and expired in 1948. The rest of the Jura system followed in 1950, showing that electric traction was not a passport to a longer life.

Happily unlike some lines, much of the route still exists with the tunnels and viaduct as good as when they were first built; most of the stations remain too so there is much still to see.

A train from St Claude at Lons-le-Saunier showing the large Bicabine locomotives used on the line. The loco has lined out panels on the front and side and must have made an attractive sight. Note the pile of briquettes plied up on top of the side tank.

In the picture below the station can be seen in the background as a train load of passengers head away towards the town. The buildings on the right beyond the gateway are the company repair shops and locomotive sheds.

Lons-le-Saunier station and depot.

The line on the right is in the direction of St Claude.

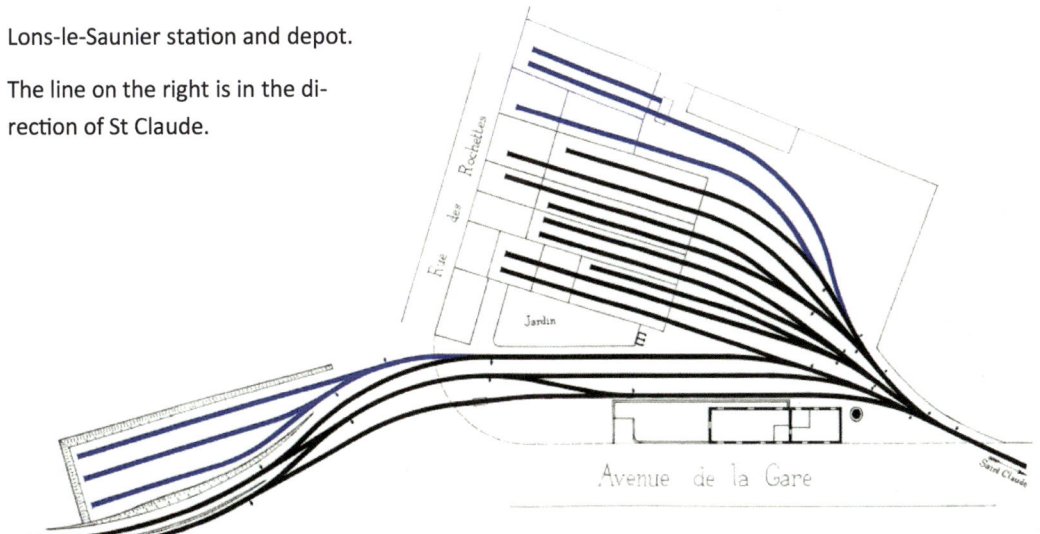

A picture taken outside the depot showing one of the large Bicabine locomotives.

The trains also stopped in the town centre as seen in these two postcards.

The town also had a station on the PLM railway line from Bourg en Bresse which opened in 1862; it became the junction of a number of lines but most have now closed leaving just the line between Strasbourg & Lyon which is single track through the station.

The postcards show a busy station in happier times.

It looks to me as though the white building above the coach in the lower pictures is the original 1862 station which has been superseded by the more ornate structure to the left which survives today.

The first station on the tramway after Lons was Perrigny, only 3km away. It was a simple affair standing alongside the road as seen here.

Remarkably the station is still there and very much unchanged though a large modern building has been constructed behind it.

The next village was Conliege where the line ran right through the middle along the streets in the usual French way.

The station was slightly outside the village; the large good shed indicates that passenger traffic was a secondary consideration here. The station building is out of the picture on the left.

The village also had a PLM station, also now closed.

That's the PLM station, high on the hillside on the left of the lower picture...at least the tramway ran through the village.

The station building at Conliege also survives as a private house.

Now we come to the main reason for including this section of line in the book, the dramatic scenery and infrastructure around the next station, Revigny. Things begin fairly placidly with this tranquil scene on the River Ornain.

The tramway crossed the Meuse on a similar girder bridge.

This is Revigny station when it was brand new in 1898; today the population is only 264 so expectations of heavy traffic would not have lasted long. The line is high on the plateau now, the station in a wind-swept location seemingly unprotected by trees. On the left is a wagon weighbridge.

The building on the left of the lower picture may be a locomotive shed.

This picture suggests that the building on the left may be a covered unloading dock; it's impossible to be sure, though a loco shed in this location is perhaps less likely.

The station is in the centre of the picture, well above the village.

Again the station building is still there, as a private house...it has been extended over the former goods shed.

This First World War picture is a charming scene.

Below is a postcard showing the challenging countryside that the line had to tackle; the tramway runs through the tunnel on the right.

This magnificent stone viaduct enabled the line to cross the valley near Revigny, a spectacular piece of engineering for a metre gauge tramway. The line may be gone but the viaduct has survived and is now part of a footpath.

38

Revigny also has a station on the PLM Paris to Stasbourg main line, though the other lines that once branched off here have been closed.

CHAPTER 4 DOMPIERRE TO ABBEVILLE

This line is the poor relation of the Somme metre gauge system; everyone knows about the coast lines but the routes inland are a lot less well known which is a shame as the lines had a lot of character. The northern section as a whole was known as the 'Reseau de Bains de Mer'.

The 31km route from Abbeville to Dompierre sur Authie opened on June 18th 1892 and served the rural communities along the route without any fuss until the inevitable closure came, on March 10th 1947 for passengers and February 1st 1951 for freight though occasional freight trains ran until 1965 when the track was lifted.

It was too far inland to attract tourist traffic and vulnerable to road competition. At Forest l'Abbaye a branch 11km long connected with the line from Noyelles station on the Nord main line from Calais but that connection with the coast lines did not generate enough passenger traffic to save the route. The branch opened on August 24th 1892 and closed with the main route.

The main outward freight was sugar beet and phosphates which were mined near Crecy and ran to Noyelles along the branch. A sugar beet factory at Crecy generated enough traffic to keep the lines open for freight when all other traffic had ceased.

This chapter will concentrate on the main line from Abbeville to Dompierre which was the terminus of the route. The intermediate stations from north to south were Wadincourt, Crecy Estrees, Foret de Crecy, Forest l'Abbaye, Lamothe-Bulaux, Canchy-Neuilly, Plessiel-Pruent, Drucat and in Abbeville Porte de Bois and Porte St Gilles.

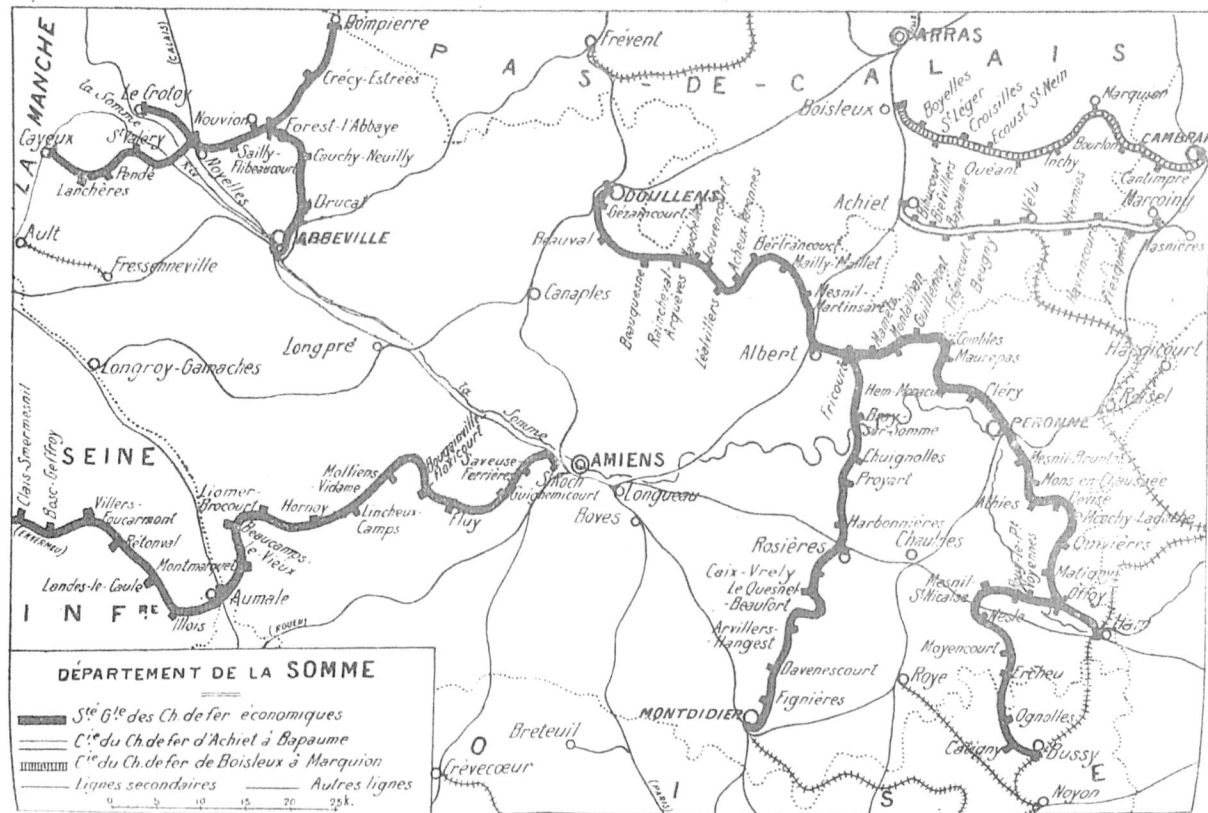

The 'Bains de Mer' system is on the top left of the map.

The terminus station of Dompierre sur Authie, disappearing under a carpet of grass around 1910. The brick station building with attached goods shed is the standard design on the Somme system and preserved examples can be seen at Cayeaux and Le Crotoy. The little town only had 545 people in 1962 which hardly qualifies it as the ideal northern terminus of the railway; today it has even fewer people. The station building is still there, as a private house.

In the lower picture a wagon can be seen on the left, standing on the loop siding that ran behind the station building.

The card below is a terrible picture but it is the only one taken from the end of the line looking back towards the station, which is hidden behind the water tower. The single track locomotive shed is on the left.

Crecy station with the locomotive of the goods train covering the area with smoke….I wonder if the photographer requested it? The main building is again brick built to the standard design.

As the lower picture shows, the goods shed was two bays long rather than the usual one reflecting the importance of this station which served both Crecy and Estrees.

High Summer at Crecy.

Close to Crecy was this 'Raperie', a factory for processing the locally grown sugar beet which was a very important crop which kept the railway going for a while after the passenger trains finished.

A short length of track remains embedded in the ground alongside the road.

The station below is Forest l'Abbeye.

Sugar beet traffic was all that kept the line going after the passenger trains finished in 1947…..trains finished in 1951 but there was still the occasional working until 1965 as seen here; a coach was not a usual part of the train.

The next station beyond Crecy was this charming structure deep in the forest, intended solely for passengers enjoying a few hours walk or a picnic in the woods. The station was far more widely photographed than the others on the line; no doubt the postcards sold well at the station.

Crécy - La halte de la forêt

The grass is reclaiming all but the running line in this later view.

Crécy-en-Ponthieu - La Buvette de la Forêt

The number of tracks here is surprising suggesting that excursion trains may have been run which were stabled here until it was time to return to Abbeville.

CRÉCY-en-PONTHIEU (Somme). - Le Chalet dans la Forêt

This is Forest l'Abbaye station, the junction for the branch to Noyelles which explains the locomotive sheds in the lower picture. The building is the standard design with the single bay goods shed attached.

That station on the southern section of the line were rarely photographed; these two pictures of Canchy are all I have of the station.

157 ABBEVILLE. — La Gare de la Porte du Bois. — LL.

In Abbeville the narrow gauge joined the route of the main line here at the station of 'Porte de Bois' and the two ran alongside towards the main line station with another stopping place at Porte St Gilles. The Nord standard gauge line is on the right beyond the level crossing barrier. The narrow gauge terminated in Abbeville station.

43. — Abbeville. La Gare

CHAPTER 5   THE MAULE TO VERSAILLES TRAMWAY

This little metre gauge tramway ran for 26km from outside the Rive Droite station in Versailles to the town of Maule, passing through St Nom de Breteche, Feucherolles and Crespieres on the way. In the manner of such lines it followed the existing road all the way; it looked perfectly at home in the little villages and at the terminus but in bustling Versailles it must have looked very much the poor relation.

The line opened in 1899 as the Tramway Versailles—Maule or TVM; a branch was built to Meulan in 1909 by way of Poissy. In 1914 the line became part of the 'CdF de Grande Banlieue' or more conveniently the CGB and by then it was considered as part of the Seine et Oise system. Passenger and goods traffic ended in 1944 though the line was not decommissioned and dismantled until 1951.

Versaillesw Rive Droite station; I am not sure where the tramway terminated. Though there are tracks crossing the setts in the foreground these may be for the electric trams serving the town centre.

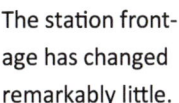

The station frontage has changed remarkably little.

As soon as it got out of Versailles the line was very much a rural roadside tramway, which is why I love it! This is the station at Saint Nom de Breteche which has a name almost as long as the little brick station building.

The train is hauled by a Pinguely 030 locomotive, with the coaches very much tramway vehicles with the clerestory roof and short length. The line on the right may be the 1909 branch to Meulan.

An unusual viewpoint for a picture of the station.

Pottering along the side of the road in the sunshine the train next arrived at Feucherolles, which also had the attractive little building in red and yellow brick bands. Mixed trains seem to have been usual.

It was a very exposed and open spot; this winter picture looks rather less appealing than the pervious one.

The large building by the station seems to be the only structure in view but hopefully the village wasn't too far away.

Presumably this briquette works would have provided traffic for the tramway.

In the final picture of the station it's Summer again and everything looks a lot more cheerful.

This tinted postcard of Crespieres station gives an excellent impression of the tramway though the locomotives were not likely to have been black; bright colours were common.

Things were a bit more developed here, with a house on the right and a wooden goods shed on the left, though in fact the house may not have been connected to the station. The tramway looks to be doing good business in this picture.

Tramway de Maule à Versailles (S.-et-O.)

The French roadside tramway captured to perfection!

The line ran through the streets of Maule towards the terminus station.

Maule — Boulevard Paul Barré

The tramway terminus had a proper station building and a goods shed, though little else. This is the best picture of one of the Pinguely 030 tank loco's and the rolling stock; the fact that one small coach was enough to cater for the expected passengers speaks for itself.

In the lower picture the main line station can be seen on the left conveniently placed for passengers transferring from one to the other. The tramway is very overgrown; money for maintenance was always hard to come by on these lines. The loco isn't very distinct, but it is not a Pinguely.

The terminus not long after it had opened and before nature began to take over; there is a well tended flower bed to the left of the coach and shrubs are growing along the trackside to the left of the station building. We tend to picture narrow gauge stations as looking fairly run down and attractively decrepit but they weren't always like that.

Below one of the Pinguely tanks waits with a bogie coach at a halt in the town centre suggesting that the line carried on past the main station to terminate here.

A couple of views of the main line station, opened on August 30th 1900 on the line from Plaisir to Mezieres. It remains open today.

This is the station at Meulan on the extension that was opened in 1909; the same style of architecture has been used for the station.

In the top picture the loco is a Pinguely again but the lower one shows a Corpet Louvet.

This is an early picture; the Corpet Louvet 030 loco is lettered 'TVM' on the buffer beam.

The lovely coloured view of Poissy on the extension to the tramway brings to an end our look at this appealing tramway.

CHAPETR 6 THE LINE OF THE EMPERORS

Staying in the same part of France with this Chapter, the railway to be described couldn't be more different; it was standard gauge and it built for the use of the highest in the land. I justify its inclusion on the grounds that it was very short indeed, and because it was extremely interesting yet very little known.

My sister lives in St Cloud, to the south west of Paris, and naturally having visited the town several times I became interested in the station. The place that you catch a train from now is a modern, functional concrete construction that gives little indication of an interesting history, but there is more to the station than meets the eye.

The line through St Cloud was an early one, the Paris to Versailles line which opened in 1839. The station was rebuilt in 1893 and given a new brick and stone station building adjacent to the tunnel mouth beyond which the line passes beneath the heights of St Cloud. The station building survives though no longer in railway use. The line became part of the Ouest system and for many years St Cloud was the second busiest station on the line after Versailles Rive Droit.

The Chateau at St Cloud was an impressive building set in rolling parkland, and in the 19th Century it was used by the Emperor. Built on the Hill de Montertout it gave a superb view over the River Seine.

In 1848 a branch line was built during the reign of Louis Phillip from St Cloud station to serve the Chateau directly. Only 400m long it left the main line before the station was reached and descended under a cut and cover tunnel over which the access road to the station passed. The branch was double track until after it had passed through the tunnel, and then single until it reached the Chateau station. This was a private station and was called 'Parks Parties Station' because it was used by revellers visiting the Chateau, but it was opened to the public on holidays and Summer weekends so that they could enjoy the grounds surrounding the chateau, something Parisians had been able to do since the revolution. The station was stone built with imposing arches and pillars, allowing passengers to detrain and walk straight into the Chateau grounds. In 1852 Napoleon 3rd moved to St Cloud to live at the Chateau, which is when the line was most heavily used.

The emperor himself had a second station which was certainly private; this was served by a separate line branching off the main line on the opposite side. The station was located west of the main line tunnel. The station was probably built for Napoleon 3rd but this is not certain; the track layout seems to have been simply two or three sidings. The station building here was a basic circular rustic wooden construction with a thatched roof on a simple platform— it was called the 'Gare de chaumes' or 'thatched station' and the contrast to the park station could not have been greater. The appearance called to mind an African roundhouse more than anything else though the sides between the wooden supports were open.

This station was strictly private and only for the use of the Emperor; across the track was a tall cast iron gate which was normally kept locked. When the Emperor's train used the station the passengers would be conveyed to the Chateau in horse drawn carriages. It was from this station that Napoleon 3rd departed for Sedan in 1870; following defeat by the Prussians he never returned to France.

In 1870 Prussian troops occupied the heights of St Cloud, and a bombardment by French artillery set fire to the Chateau which was totally destroyed along with the station on October 13th 1870. Remarkably both lines remained in place until 1930, at which time the tunnel was declared unsafe. The remains were sold to the local authority, the track was removed and the tunnel demolished along with what was left of the Park station; a school now occupies the site. The Thatched station was on the site now occupied by a sub station serving the main line and may have been used in 1928 to move materials before being dismantled.

The main line was electrified using the third rail in 1928 after which the station remained largely unchanged until 1964 when the station building was replaced with a concrete structure on the other side of the line, together with new canopies, access ramps and a footbridge….fortunately the original station building was not demolished and is still there today in use as offices. The line was electrified with overhead catenary throughout, and the station now had two island platforms to give greater flexibility in working. The station remains busy, though the procession of electric units is not very inspiring for the enthusiast!

My thanks to Geoffrey Nickson of the SNCF Society for help with this chapter.

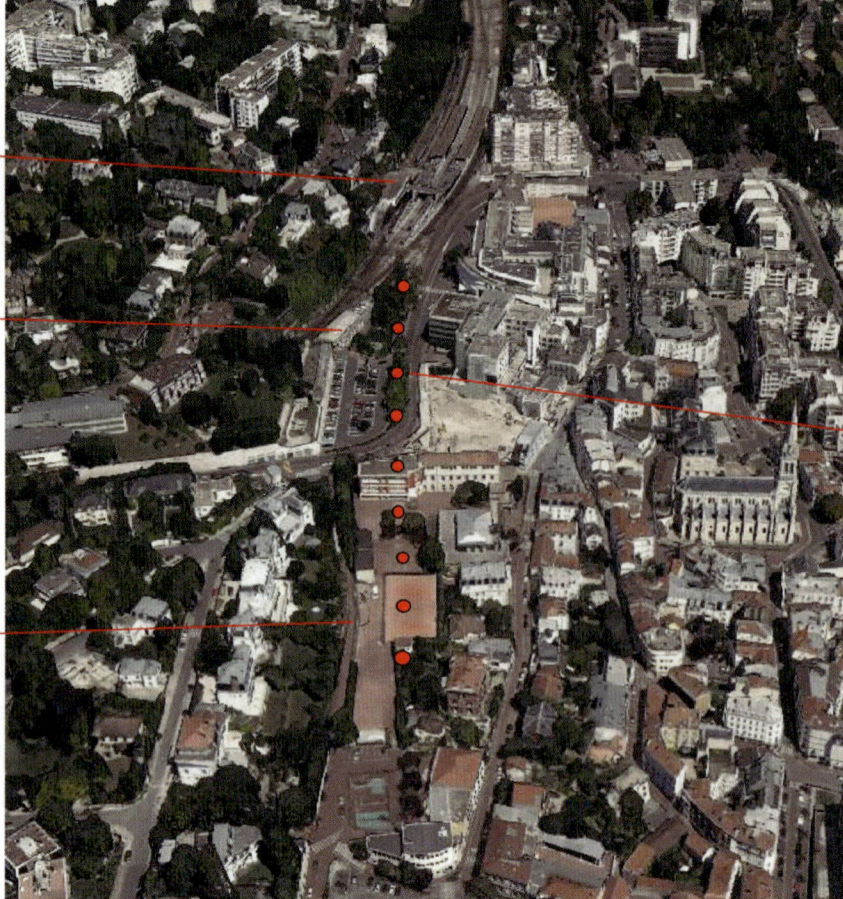

A view over St Cloud showing the park and the Chateau with the town beyond, probably in the 18th century.

This map clearly shows the line to the 'Gare de Fetes' but the Emperor's private station is not shown.

French postcards all blame the Prussians for setting fire to the Chateau, but in fact it was artillery from French troops that began the fire!

The painting above by Edouard Dantan shows the original St Cloud station of 1839; he sat in gardens above the tunnel mouth to paint the picture during 1880 which shows an Ouest 'Bicyclette' 120 loco on a train which includes a double deck carriage behind the Fourgon.

In 1893 the station building was replaced with the one shown below which survives today.

A view of the 1893 station showing he branch to the 'Gare de Fetes' passing under the tunnel and the pointwork by which it became single track for the remainder of the 400m distance to the terminus. The junction with the main line was beyond the main line station platforms.

The shallow tunnel over which the approach road passed became unsafe which was the reason for demolishing the tunnel and removing the branch in 1930. The area is almost unrecognisable today.

In the picture below the branch can clearly be seen running below the two bridges, descending quite steeply towards the terminus. The main line is on the right at a much higher level with the line running into the tunnel on the extreme right of the picture. The branch may have been short but it cannot have been cheap to build.

These are the ruins of the 'Gare de Fetes' around 1900. They were not demolished until 1930.

On the right is the 1893 station building, in excellent condition and in use as offices.

The 1964 rebuilding resulted in a functional but uninspiring station. The 1893 station building is to the left of the tunnel mouth in the above picture.

CHAPTER 7   VOIRON

Voiron was the terminus of the metre gauge tramway from Saint-Beron, traversing the Savoie and Isere departments. It was 35km long, opening in 1895 and closing on September 30th 1936. This chapter is going to concentrate on the Voiron area as it makes an ideal prototype for modellers looking for a station serving both standard gauge and metre gauge routes.

The narrow gauge lines shared the main line station at Voiron, the line then climbing alongside the standard gauge until it gained enough height to cross it on a girder bridge before heading north into the mountains. The standard gauge line is the PLM route from Lyon and Perrache to Grenoble, the first part of which was opened in 1856.

As seen in the first picture, the two gauges shared a platform so it was ideal for passengers changing between the two routes.

The station remains open and still has the original PLM buildings.

In the lower picture the station is on the right; the narrow gauge lines were on the far side, the area to the right of the road is the PLM goods yard.

The tramway climbed into the mountains seen in the background; it must have been one of the finest rides in the whole of France.

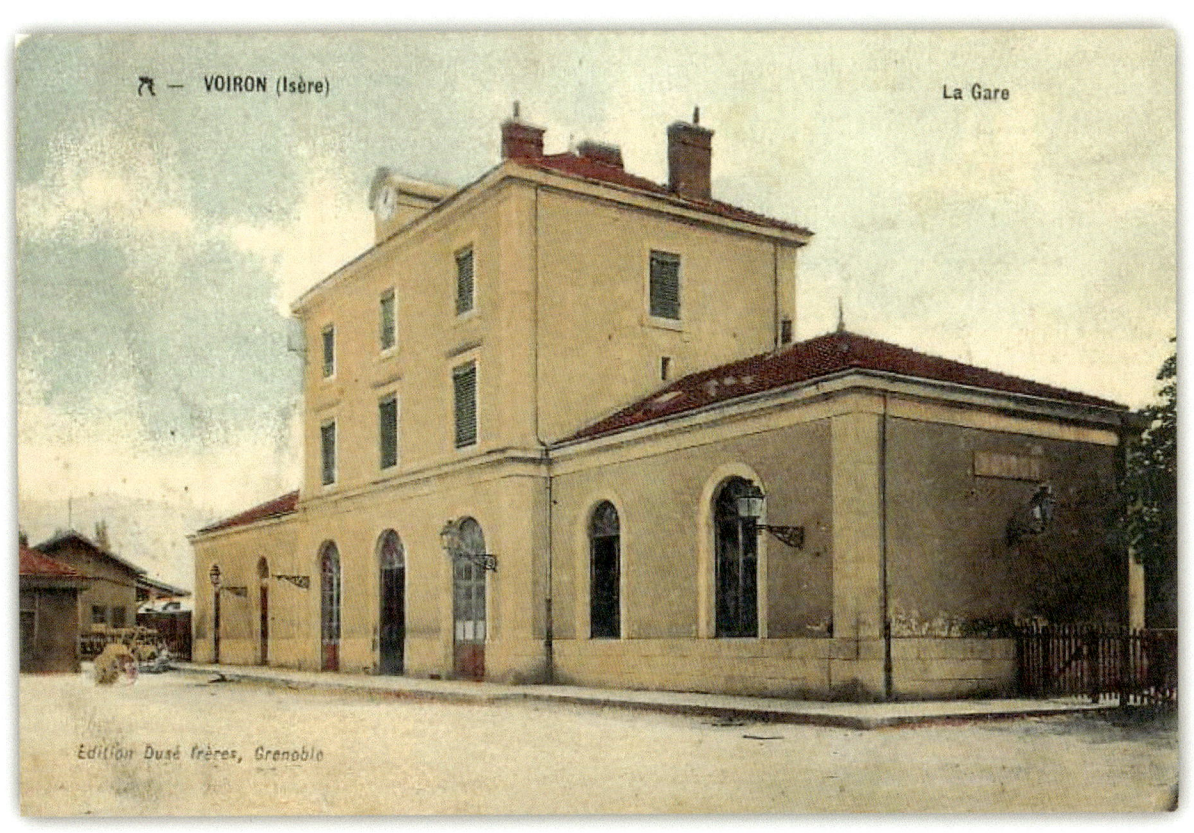

The tramway climbed quite steeply away from the station, running alongside the PLM line until it had gained sufficient height to cross it on this girder bridge, after which the lines headed in different directions. The tramway route was to the north through the mountains.

20 DE l'OIRON A LA GRANDE CHARTREUSE. — *Les Gorges de Chailles.* — LL.

The line climbed into the rugged Massif de Chartreuse, following the road as much as possible but having to tunnel though this projection of rock.

599. DAUPHINÉ — Massif de la Chartreuse - Les Gorges de Crossey - Le Tunnel

It really was a spectacular route; fortunately the postcard publishers realised the potential of the dramatic scenery with the tiny train somewhere in the picture.

107. Environs de VOIRON — Les gorges du Crossey et la Grande Sure

ÉTÉ 1910

Voiron, St-Laurent-du-Pont, St-Béron

Distances de Voiron	PRIX des PLACES de Voiron aux gares ci-après		Départs de Lyon....... Grenoble....	matin	matin 6 50 8 15 matin	matin 9 55 9 31 matin	matin 11 56 11 47 matin	soir 5 30 3 29 soir	matin 12 02 4 07 matin	soir » 10 23 soir
			Heures d'arrivée à Voiron des trains P.-L.-M et C.E.N venant de	Lyon..... Grenoble.. Charavines	matin » 6 52 6 45 matin	matin » 8 57 » matin	soir 9 31 12 29 10 33 soir	soir 11 12 4 08 » soir	soir 3 24 7 25 7 03 soir	matin 7 45 4 48 » matin	soir 3 14 10 20 10 05 (2)
	1re	2e	**NOMS DES GARES**			**TRAINS RÉGULIERS**			**T. S.**	
				3	5	7(3)	9	11	13	15(1) 17(1)
				matin	matin	matin	soir	soir	soir	matin soir
»	»	»	Voiron......départ	»	7 02	9 45	12 45	4 25	7 56	4 52 10 30
3	0 30	0 15	La Buisse.....(*)	»	7 10	9 53	12 53	4 34	8 04	4 59 10 38
4	0 35	0 25	Coublevie........	»	7 15	9 58	12 58	4 40	8 09	5 03 10 43
6	0 55	0 35	Croix-Bayard......(*)	»	7 20	10 03	1 03	4 46	8 14	5 08 10 48
9	0 75	0 45	Saint-Étienne-de-Cros	»	7 29	10 12	1 12	4 55	8 23	5 17 10 57
13	1 10	0 70	Pont-de-Demay...(*)	»	7 44	10 27	1 27	5 11	8 38	5 31 11 12
15	1 30	0 80	Saint-Joseph-de-Rivière	»	7 50	10 33	1 33	5 17	8 44	5 36 11 17
18	1 65	1 »	Le Cotterg......(*)	»	7 56	10 39	1 39	5 24	8 50	5 42 11 23
19	1 65	1 »	St-Laurent-Pt-Ville.	»	8 02	10 44	1 44	5 30	8 55	5 47 11 28
19	1 65	1 »	S-Laurent-d-P.Rev. ar. d.	matin 5 52	8 04	10 46	1 46	5 32	8 57	5 49 11 30
23	2 05	1 25	Aiguenoire.....(*)	6 00	8 16	10 56	1 50	5 46	9 04	matin soir
25	2 20	1 35	Entre-deux-Guiers(*)	6 08	8 24	11 04	1 58	6 03	9 12	
25	2 20	1 35	Les Échelles.....	6 16	8 31	11 12	2 05	6 15	9 18	
28	2 60	1 60	La Croix de la Roche.(*)	6 22	8 35	11 20	2 10	6 25	»	
29	2 60	1 60	Chailles.........	6 26	8 41	11 26	2 15	6 31	»	
35	3 15	1 95	Saint-Béron....arrivée	6 46	9 05	11 50	2 40	6 35	»	
			Heures de départ de St Béron des trains P.-L.-M. et T.-P.-B. allant à	Lyon..... Chambéry. Pont-de- Beauvoisin	matin 7 02 7 22 7 04 matin	matin 9 37 9 17 9 42 matin	soir 1 00 12 06 1 02 soir	soir 4 26 2 58 2 55 soir	soir 8 10 7 42 8 10 soir	» » »	» » »
			Arrivée à Lyon........ — à Chambéry.... — Aix-les-Bains..	matin 9 06 8 00 8 30 matin	matin 11 47 9 58 11 04 matin	soir 3 34 12 46 4 13 soir	soir 6 58 3 39 4 43 soir	soir 11 13 8 24 9 11 soir	» » »	» » »

CHEMIN DE FER DES Quatre-Chemins A VOIRON

ARRÊTÉ

désignant les territoires qui doivent être traversés par le Chemin de fer

ARRÊTONS :

ARTICLE PREMIER. — Les territoires sur lesquels seront exécutés les travaux du Chemin de fer des Quatre-Chemins à Voiron dans le département de l'Isère sont, conformément au plan général approuvé, savoir :

Dans l'arrondissement de Saint-Marcellin, ceux des communes de Saint-Blaise-de-Buis, La Murette, Réaumont et Saint-Cassien ;

Et dans l'arrondissement de Grenoble, celui de la commune de Voiron.

ARTICLE 2. — Le présent arrêté sera publié à son de trompe ou de caisse dans chacune des communes ci-dessus désignées, et y sera affiché, tant à la principale porte de l'église qu'à celle de la mairie, par les soins et à la diligence de MM. les Maires. Il sera, en outre, inséré dans les journaux *Le Patriote des Alpes* et *Le Mémorial de Saint-Marcellin* du treize mai mil huit cent quatre-vingt-quatorze, lesquels se publient à Grenoble et à Saint-Marcellin.

Fait et arrêté à Grenoble, en l'hôtel de la Préfecture, le dix-huit avril mil huit cent quatre-vingt-quatorze.

Pour le Préfet de l'Isère :

Le Secrétaire Général délégué,

Signé : H. PERRET.

Pour ampliation :

Le Conseiller de Préfecture,

Signé : MOTTET.

OBSERVATIONS. — (1) *Les trains nos 15, 17 et 18 ont lieu les Jeudis, Dimanches et Fêtes du 1er Juin au 15 Septembre inclus.* — (2 Le train de 10 h 10 soir, allant à Charavines n'a lieu que les Dimanches et Fêtes du 14 juillet au 11 septembre inclus. — (3) Les trains nos 7 et 8 sont supprimés à partir du 6 Octobre entre St-Béron et Entre-deux-Guiers. — (0) Le train de 10 h. 13. (ouvrières) a lieu les Dimanches et jours de fêtes légales et prend des voyageurs en 3e classe à Voiron pour Moirans et Grenoble.

(*) *Haltes ouvertes aux voyageurs sans bagages.* — Dans le cas où des voyageurs auraient des bagages de ou pour ces haltes, ils seraient obligés de les présenter eux-mêmes au fourgon ou de les réclamer au fourgon contre remise immédiate de leur bulletin ; dans ce cas les bagages sont toujours enregistrés pour la gare suivante, ou de la gare précédente avec billets pris pour la gare suivante, ou de la gare précédente.

(*) Les trains ne s'arrêtent aux haltes qu'autant qu'il y a des voyageurs à prendre ou à laisser. — Les voyageurs du train doivent prévenir les chefs de train et ceux qui sont dans les haltes faire signe aux mécaniciens.

CHAPTER 8   THE LAGNY TO MORTCERF TRAMWAY

Back to the flatlands for this chapter, a little tramway that became part of the Seine et Marne system. It began life connecting the town of Lagny, on the south bank of the Marne east of Paris, with Villeneuve le Compte 12km away by way of what is now the D231 road, passing through the village of Serris on the way. This line opened in 1872 so it was an early example of a metre gauge roadside tramway; in 1902 it was extended a further 8km to Mortcerf where it terminated not far from the main line station.

It opened early and closed early, in 1934, the victim as ever of more efficient road transport. It amazes me that such a rural tramway can have existed so close to the metropolis of Paris, but it did.

This is the view the intending passenger would have of Lagny station; it looks odd until you remember that it was a terminus and the station building is at right angles to the tracks which ran parallel with the road...in fact they were to follow the road for most of the route.

Remarkably the scene hasn't changed much since the line closed in 1934. The station building has been extended and is now a private house.

80

The station was on the Rue St Denis in Lagny. I am not sure where the tracks in the foreground went; possibly to the loco sheds or goods yard which would have been built on flat ground.

The loco in the lower picture is a Pinguely 030 tank.

The intermediate station at Serris, another of those little roadside stations far from the village it served.

The station is on the left in the lower picture behind the row of trees.

4 — **Serris** - Gare départementale   Morville, édit. - Serris

It looks a lot bleaker in this mid Winter view though plenty of people have turned out for the picture. A passing loop seems to been the extent of the track here.

Villeneuve le Comte was the terminus of the line from 1872 to 1902 and the station barely changed when the extension was built. Most of the facilities are seen here; all the loco sheds seem to have been at Lagny. The photographer had the knack of attracting large crowds of children!

Villeneuve-le-Comte — Arrivée d'un train

The village school on the left might explain all the children in the previous picture!

The area is very flat and featureless; agricultural produce accounted for a high proportion of the line's traffic.

A 130 locomotive at the 1902 terminus station at Mortcerf; mixed trains would have been usual on a line such as t is.

The lower view shows the adjacent main line station in the background.

This factory seems to have generated traffic for the tramway but I have no record of what was produced there.

This is the attractive Est station, basking in the Summer sun. The trees would have provided welcome shade.

Happily the Est station is still open and has the original station building in excellent condition.

CHAPTER 9 CHAMARET TO TAULIGNAN

This independent tramway was again metre gauge and was situated in the Drome region. Opened in 1907 it connected the PLM line at Chamaret with the towns of Grignan and Taulignan 11km away. The local authority took over the company in 1925 as it was struggling financially but the change was unable to save the line which closed in 1928, well before most narrow gauge lines gave up the ghost. The official abandonment was in 1932.

The tramway only ever had two locomotives, both Corpet Louvet 030 tanks, works numbers 1129 and 1130. The fact that there was only one coach says something about the numbers of passengers using the line!

There is a danger that these little railways disappear into the mists of time unrecorded and unnoticed ; hopefully this chapter will ensure that this line at least is remembered.

This is the terminus station at Taulignan with one of the two Corpet Louvet tanks ready to leave. Facilities were pretty minimal. Because the background has been painted out it is hard to pin down just where the station was, but it seems to have been on the edge of the town with the line continuing to terminate in the main square where just a small shelter was provided.

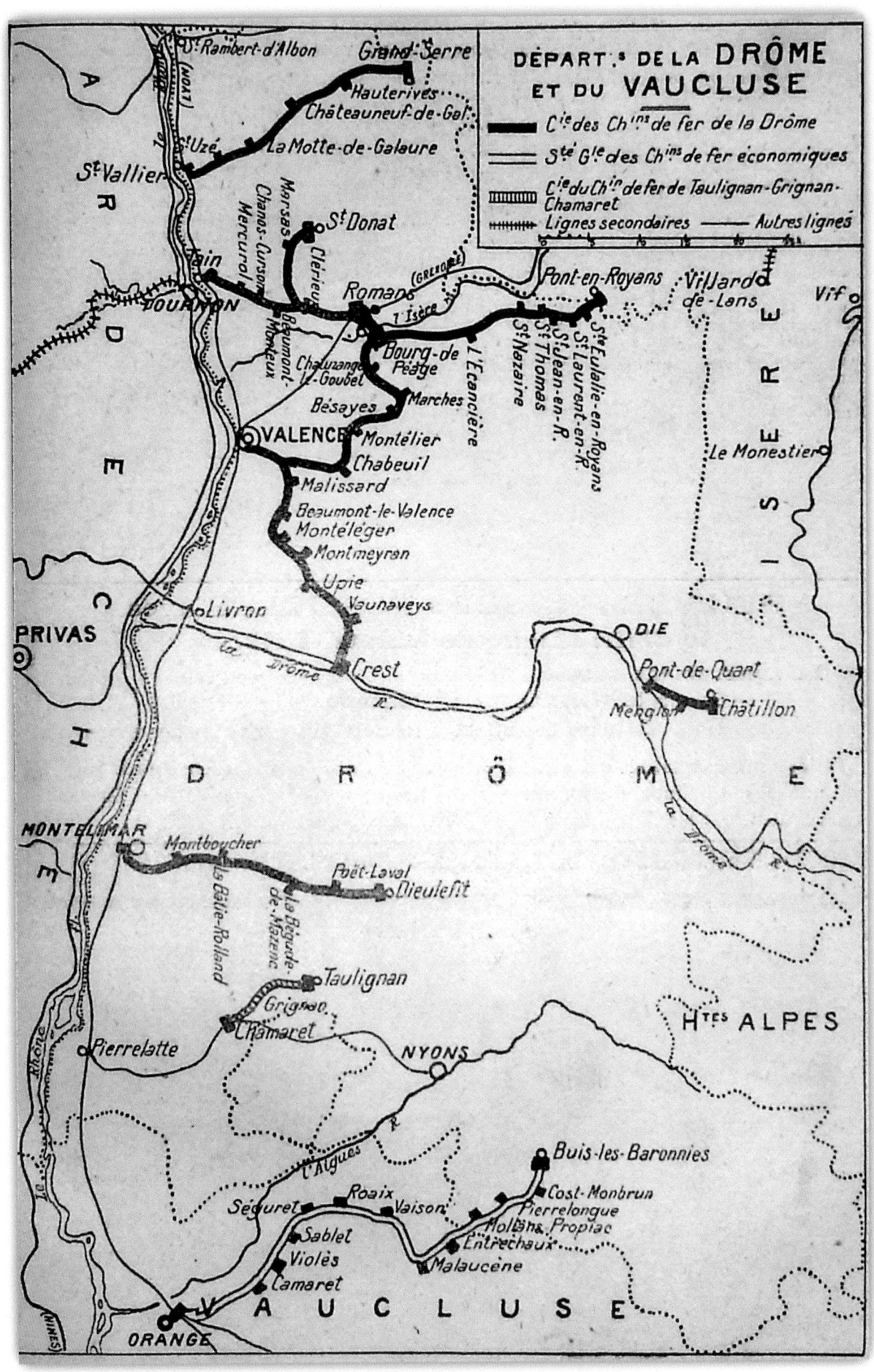

A second view of the station on the edge of the town, soon after opening judging by the immaculate locomotive. The pile of briquettes on the raised platform by the station building suggests that the building on the left may be a locomotive shed.

The postcard below shows the whole of the town; a place such as this was never likely to generate enough traffic to keep the tramway going for long after World War One. The line terminated in the triangular area on the lower right of the picture—the large building is a school.

The entire passenger stock owned by the company is posed proudly at Taulignan.

This station was the actual end of the line, right in the town square, with the main station on the edge of town where there was more space to deal with freight. The structure in the picture above that looks like a water tower is actually part of the school building at the side of the square as the small picture makes clear.

You couldn't accuse the tramway of not being convenient for the town centre!

The only intermediate station on the line was at Grignan.

This is a true hilltop town so it is understandable that the tramway station was at the bottom of the hill but it would have been a stiff walk from the station into the town.

It certainly makes an impressive backdrop to the pictures.

The connection to the outside world was at Chamaret where the station was adjacent to the PLM facilities.

The PLM station can be seen on the right; opened in 1897 this was on the line from Pierrelatte to Nyons which closed in 1951 when a canal broke its banks and washed away the track; no money could be found for repairs and abandonment was confirmed in 1954.

The tramway looks very basic, with minimal structures; there must have been a loco shed somewhere here if the structure at Taulignan wasn't it.

The PLM station in about 1910.

Those few pictures are probably the only ones that were taken of the tramway; it's a meagre collection but I love these obscure little railways so I wanted to include them.

My thanks to the members of www.ngrm-online.com for their help with this chapter.

You might also enjoy these books, all available from Amazon:

FRENCH MINOR RAILWAYS Vol 1

NARROW GAUGE INSPIRATION 1

NARROW GAUGE INSPIRATION 2

NARROW GAUGE INSPIRATION 3

THE THONES—ANNECY TRAMWAY

THE THIZY TRAMWAY

NARROW GAUGE ON THE ILE DE RE.

SCRATCHBUILT BUILDINGS THE KIRTLEY WAY

MODELLING SCENERY THE KIRTLEY WAY

Printed in Great Britain
by Amazon.co.uk, Ltd.,
Marston Gate.